T0149404

The Bittersweet Journey

A Collection of Poetic Sketches

Nancy L. Martinez

AuthorHouse™
1663 Liberty Drive
Bloomington, IN 47403
www.authorhouse.com
Phone: 1-800-839-8640

Published by AuthorHouse 10/09/2014

ISBN: 978-1-4969-3837-4 (sc)
ISBN: 978-1-4969-3836-7 (e)

This book is printed on acid-free paper.

Acknowledgements

First and foremost, I thank God for the inspiration and healing He has done in my life. I would not choose any other life than the life my God has given me. I will use the rest of my years to proclaim His power and mercy to those who love Him and seek Him.

I would like to thank my family members, especially my parents, Tom and Mary Martinez. They have been married 52 years and raised me to become the God fearing woman I am today. My family is always there for one another. I love all of you!!

I would like to acknowledge my largest supporter in life next to my mother, DeAnna Montoya-Garduno. She is the most patient, loving, and generous person I know outside of my family. DeAnna, you have truly become my spiritual sister. Thank you for all your support.

I would also like to thank Joseph Ulibarri as he patiently listened to many pieces as they were coming together and offered continued encouragement. Thank you for those times and I hope you have the life you have been searching for. I wish you the best through the Love of Christ.

Acknowledgments

[illegible]

[illegible]

[illegible]

[illegible]

Contents

Prelude

This poetic collection was compiled to reach those who have no hope, those whose lives have been surrounded by darkness or depression. The dialect is based on my experiences, and this collection documents my journey in life through a poetic, artistic medium. Combined with scripture from the Holy Bible, the pilgrimage begins with darkness and concludes with light.

The beginnings of these poems are consumed by darkness because of the obscure and disheartened life I led since my childhood. The very first section are poems I begin to write at about 11 years old. However, it is obvious my life was completely changed throughout the years.

This is a journey of redemption captured in the form of poetic sketches, which portray thoughts, feelings, ideas, dreams, and sorrow. Even though there is darkness, these writings also observe different aspects humans endure throughout a lifetime. It is a commemoration of life, love, and pain. I specifically mention pain, because if we did not experience such emotional hurt, we would not be who we are today.

As I escaped the darkness, I was transformed only by the power of God. I know this change is possible for anyone through a spiritual and personal relationship with Jesus Christ. His love and manifestation in my life continues to grow with every passing day.

Each of the poems in this collection will display a scripture from the Bible, as well as a personal quote of insight to help decipher the meaning. Even though each poem has its own inspiration, all the pieces are written to be subject to the reader's interpretation. Understanding the sections is about discovering the meaning each personally speaks to the reader. When the individual meaning is revealed, the potential for new perceptive and growth is instilled. It is important to remember these writings represent art displayed in words. They can be considered an audible vision describing overall salvation. As with any art form, the poems are created to develop personal insight and move one's philosophy of life to a different level.

I recognize many people will feel the emotions painted in each poem. This is a bittersweet journey of a life similar to many, a life of vague reality and the light at the end of the tunnel. Although some pieces may not seem to have closure, keep in mind this collection is one entire collage of words describing the transformation from darkness to light using my life as an example. If one section does not provide meaning, look to another to fully understand. It is there you will find the story.

Please be aware that the following poetic pieces are not about a religion, but a relationship with Jesus Christ. It is about a Savior who died for all of us. This book is not intended to be an invitation to religion, but an example of the power of God to transform even the darkest of lives. Although my beliefs are based on Christianity, please remember Jesus Christ wants a personal relationship with us, rather than merely conforming to a certain religion.

Jesus Christ gives hope to a world filled with darkness. He will lift the darkness and use even the darkest of moments to provide hope. This book is an example of the power of God and his use of my previous state of darkness to reveal a testimony of overcoming the dark moments, and the light replacing the desolation. It is my hope you will find the peace He has provided in my life. Remember, if you identify with the despair in the beginning of the book, you are not alone. Many people are bound by feelings of misery and depression. However, Jesus Christ is also willing to be right by your side. Just accept His love and mercy. Read the prayer at the end of the book, seek God, fellowship with other believers, and you, too, can also receive the beauty of darkness to light. You can then begin your own journey of emotional healing.

For I know the plans I have for you," declares the LORD, "plans to prosper you and not to harm you, plans to give you hope and a future."

Jeremiah 29:11 (NIV)

Frozen Darkness

Trust in the Lord with all your heart, And lean not on your own understanding; In all your ways acknowledge Him, And He shall direct your paths.
Proverbs 3:5-6 (NKJV)

Then Jesus spoke to them again, saying, "I am the light of the world. He who follows Me shall not walk in darkness, but have the light of life."
John 8:12 (NKJV)

Walking in darkness can have various meanings to different people. Darkness in this section mainly refers to depression and emptiness in life. Several of the pieces describe a life of torment. The interesting part of this section is that all the poems were written before the age of twenty and the first was written at age 11. Even as a child I was filled with feelings of self-condemnation.

Although some may say we should not look at the darkness we came out of, I believe we need to look at where we were at in order to be grateful for where we are. The only danger in looking back is dwelling on the past instead of learning from it. I realize now I am an overcomer in Christ, and I never want to be in that type of darkness again.

Don't become distracted by the pain, but look to the answer which lies on the opposite page of each piece. You may either identify with the emotional hurt, or you may know someone who does. Either way, the message is about the power of God, and the ability He has to save the hopeless.

STILL

Storm clouds gather.
A downpour of rain.
Drops trickle down the façade we all hold;
The surface is now clean,
but underneath indifference will remain.
Endless winds softly blow over the infinite shores.
We are all a little piece of grain on this beach of eternity;
Looking up at heaven's unlocked doors.
Now we stand in the shadow of authenticity, holding on to doubt.
The flame that burned within is slowly going out.
Foolishly seeking protection in a diminishing star;
The journey to peace is still so far.

Be still, and know that I am God.

Psalms 46:10 (NKJV)

During the storm, it is not easy to be still and patient. In the long run, the most effective act we can do is to *wait upon the Lord.*

BLIND

In the midst of the darkness;
A wavering spirit, a confused soul;
Foolishly allowed someone else to take control.
Whenever it appears someone will care;
I reach out only to embrace thin air.
Before me the kind stranger disappeared;
Now coming true is all I feared.

Some say things will change if I close my eyes, pray and wait;
But all I see are the bleeding memories that tell of my fate.
They quietly whisper things of the painful past,
Remind me that I was undeserving
of love and happiness will never last.
They show me whoever I trusted was someone who lied.
I remember the hurtful words that stole my pride.

Even though I understand these memories
are now only etched in time,
I face the fact they will always be mine.
I no longer want to be a foreigner to my own mind,
But I will continue on my path
because the darkness has already rendered me blind.

I will bring the blind by a way they did not know; I will lead them in paths they have not known. I will make darkness light before them, and crooked places straight. These things I will do for them, and not forsake them.

Isaiah 42:16 (NKJV)

We are often blinded to the truth of a situation. Pain creates a vulnerability to this kind of blindness. These types of situations can be emotionally hurtful. Seek guidance from the only one who knows the truth and is the truth-Jesus Christ.

POINT OF VIEW

Slowly the shadowy secrets enclose;
The paralyzing pain it appears no one else knows.
Constantly seeking refuge from the thunder and storm,
In search for the love that never took form.

Unable to sleep in the dead of night,
Nightmares reveal the true sight.
Only suffering will extend a hand;
Few seem to understand.

Condemned to a life of solitude,
Enduring rejection with neither a conclusion nor prelude.
Just when it seems there is nothing but the point of decay,
Renewed forgiveness is bestowed upon the day.

The healing light of salvation is cast;
Momentarily there seems to be hope at last.
However, the myth of happy endings has yet to come true,
But it all depends upon your point of view.

I will not leave you comfortless: I will come to you.
John 14:18 (KJV)

In times of trouble we may feel as though we are alone and no comfort is in sight. God is our comforter and refuge. He is the author of true happy endings.

SKETCH OF LIFE

I built my house on a foundation of despondency,
Guarded by walls of thickened misery.
The ground is frozen with bitterness that continues to linger,
The sky blackened with layers of anger.

Life had become the tomb of death,
Though the cadaver has not yet taken her last breath.
Blinded by tears, running with no destination in mind;
Resting during the night in the first fallen star I find.

I continued on this shameful path and passed the cities,
the ruins, the forest, and the trees;
Accused of treason and brought to my knees.
Searching in vain through the blind man's eyes,
Complacently shielded by my convivial disguise.

I breathe to remember I am still alive;
I bleed to remember death can arrive.
I flee because I know I am not immune;
I turn away because I loved much too soon.

Here it is: The Blank Canvas.
Be it filled with love or be it filled with strife,
I give to you my sketch of life.

Come to me, all who are weary and burdened, and I will give you rest.

Matthew 11:28 (NIV)

No matter how hard we try, we cannot run from ourselves. True peace and rest can only be found in God.

THE ONE YOU KNOW

I've let the earth embrace my heart,
Drop the moonlight to illuminate my path.
Always traveling my journey with caution,
Painstakingly stricken with unexpected aftermath.
My eyes so easily overflow with tears;
I have carried the weary child;
Still holding her resonating fears.
Bitterly reaping what I foolishly sow;
My faith has reluctantly failed me;
My blood gleams against the winter snow.

Look at me now. *Am I the one you know?*

I've been kissed by the friendly sun;
Wrapped in the comfort of the quiet moon;
Holding on to adolescent beliefs because I grew up too soon.
Look downward at my flesh; see the scars inflicted by strife,
Wounds created by the bitter sharpness I have learned to call life.
I am merely trying to survive, and I am not your foe.

Look at me now. *Am I the one you know?*

Torn apart by blood, united by tragedy;
Hardly befriended by my perfect family.
I will continue on my bittersweet path alone.

Look at me now. *Am I the one you've known?*

This then is how we know that we belong to the truth, and how we set our hearts at rest in his presence whenever our hearts condemn us. For God is greater than our hearts, and he knows everything.

1 John 3:19-20 (NIV)

We think we can hide all of our faults from everyone. We believe no one knows us, but God knows us better than we know ourselves.

SURVIVAL

Starved in a famine of affection,
My skeletons have become a substitute for you.

Considering your love to be a placebo;
Engrained so deep I believe its effects to be true.

I asked you once to love me, lest the poison tear us apart.
Please do not slow my spirit, nor place reins upon my heart.

You may not see the life-giving metaphor
that will never inflict pain and will never fail;
Seducing my logic in an attempt to dissuade
my self-designed fairy-tale.

I waited patiently for you near the prison gate;
Hoping I was not too late.

Leave me as I am; Love me though I am not.
Otherwise, think of me as a displaced afterthought.

I will still search for the placid words only you can speak-
Disillusionment I learned from the meek.

In the end I was blindly mistaken as to enchant and enthrall,
Only to find this is the beginning of my survival.

My flesh and my heart may fail, but God is the strength of my heart and my portion forever.

Psalms 73:26 (NIV)

Letting go of someone, even if it is an unhealthy relationship, can be painful. However, God is the only one we never have to let go of. He will always be there for us when we turn to Him. He will guide us through our emotional battles, and eventually we will learn that true survival is only possible through Jesus Christ.

THE INNOCENCE

The Innocence has become a shadow; cold and untouchable.
It is the part of my life that was never available.
The Innocence was once sought by most and by others held dear.
To some it is a gift; to myself it became unsettled drear.

They all quietly partook of my essence, leaving me to bleed;
As if they were children, and had the right to feed.
The frailties will linger, as will vivid memories of conventional sin;
Potent images with messages of w*hat should have been.*

Call it ignorance or acceptance; label it as you will.
Either way, it was highly influenced by those who were volatile.
You may dwell on the shortcomings, the mistakes, and the pain.
Stand in your own life or make your own rain.

This can be loss or liberation, no longer blind and naïve.
One must decide when to close the chapter and prepare to leave.
I have chosen liberation and I believe what I choose to believe;
Because in the end- the lack of innocence has created me.

The thief does not come except to steal, and to kill, and to destroy. I have come that they may have life, and that they may have it more abundantly.

John 10:10 (NIV)

Many people are robbed of a childhood because of abuse. This abuse can take any form and many are left to repair the damage resulting from the pain. Jesus Christ can and will bring comfort to the afflicted. There is life after abuse, but the wounds are only and truly healed through our Lord Jesus Christ.

THE DREAM

You have touched my open wounds;
Run your fingers across my scars.
Within my eyes you have seen the Son;
Within my smile you have seen the stars.

I hold tight to the beliefs created when I was young.
Each belief I never chose;
Challenge the beliefs I have learned as an adult.
My dream is the belief no one knows.

I live in a dream as most people do.
In this dream I am paying a lifetime for each mistake.
My dream becomes a nightmare—
A place from which I never wake.

I am ruled by faith;
But governed by fear.
Ashamed and alone;
My life is displayed within every tear.

As I now walk through my river and listen,
Will I believe you or believe what I feel?
My dream will always show itself in my life,
But only God, in His time, will show what is real.

Much dreaming and many words are meaningless. Therefore stand in awe of God.

Ecclesiastes 5:7 (NIV)

As humans we will have dreams revealed unconsciously and dreams we have for our lives. Either way, God should be allowed to be in control of both. We can then watch the power of God work in our lives and freely stand in awe of the outcomes.

Seeking Solace in my Broken Promises

Blessed is she who has believed that the Lord would fulfill his promises to her!"

Luke 1:45 (NIV)

For he has not despised or scorned the suffering of the afflicted one; he has not hidden his face from him but has listened to his cry for help.

Psalm 22:24 (NIV)

When life appears bleak and empty, we seek avenues such as relationships, achievement, addiction, and anything else which will momentarily distract from the pain. There is no perfect relationship other than the relationship with Jesus Christ. There is also no amount of money or status that can replace the peace God offers. This section addresses the loss surrounding some of these issues and forgiveness associated with the mistakes and acts of desperation.

The pieces written for this section were more of a cry for help through the loneliness. During a time when no one else heard my cry, God did. His faithfulness proved to be steadfast as He sustained me during this time.

JUDGEMENT DAY

I look up as the darkness surrounds me.
I watch the light helplessly shrink from my reach.
I lie on the frozen ground and listen to my heartbeat
as it slows to a standstill.
I know we are usually blinded by brightness,
imprisoned by darkness, and we rarely enjoy the twilight.
I must admit my season appears to have come to an end.

As I lay on the cold ground, my mind drifts
to the afterlife and Judgment day.
I meagerly gather my shards of personal verdicts,
eyes downward with shame.
I will be asked how I cared
for the inner child that was given to me;
I will have to admit that I could not nurture her
because I could not give what I never had.

As she lay gasping for air in my arms,
my own tears fall upon her face;
Knowing her wounds could not be healed
because I was blinded by love, driven by hate, and
harbored a bitterness that covered my soul like October frost.
In a world that yields no mercy for the weak, I am alone and bare.

In truth, the once beautiful Spanish Rose has truly wilted
from a thirst for affection and hunger for love.
Her last petal holds on, afraid of falling to the ground.
There is no room in the world for an empty person such as I;
Because I was already condemned to fall.

Therefore, there is now no condemnation for those who are in Christ Jesus.

Romans 8:1 (NIV)

When relationships with other people dissolve, many will blame themselves. No matter what the situation, there is no condemnation in Christ.

ENGRAVED IN TIME

I have walked along the dagger's edge,
Turning away from the alluring ledge.
Traveling my obscure path alone,
Searching for a place to call my own.

You gently took my spirit by the hand,
Showed me truth without demand.
Kissed me and caressed me with words alone.
Perennial bliss I have never known.
My soul you have enchanted,
My heart's desire granted.
Together we would wade through reverie.
I finally found some serenity.

Unexpectedly faced with once upon a time;
Painstakingly accepted you could not be mine.
Secretly, I wished for happily ever after,
Left with fading memories of our distant laughter.
Whimsical, ardent affection;
Now becomes a withered reflection.
Call it love, vulnerability, or even call it fate;
I close my eyes and let it all dissipate.

You helped me feel again, but now my heart retreats to stone.
Once more I will continue on my path alone.
Still haunted by your beautiful voice,
As it echoes with its resonating chime.
My darling, please remember;
My love for you will always be engraved in time.

I will give them an undivided heart and put a new spirit in them; I will remove from them their heart of stone and give them a heart of flesh.

Ezekiel 11:19 (NIV)

It may seem that we have found the perfect person to fulfill our lives, but then something goes terribly wrong, and we are alone again. The only perfect person there ever was and ever will be is Jesus Christ. If you have experienced this, seek a personal relationship with Jesus and find your identity in Him. The hurt will take time to heal, but now you have a comforter.

THE DOOR OF GOODBYE

Along came the thunder and storm,
As you held the expectation that I would conform.
I slowly carved your initials into my heart,
As I quietly prayed we would never part.
Now it's been a while since I sought your affection.
I looked into your eyes and no longer saw my reflection.
I waited patiently for your last kiss.
Instead, I fell in love with my bitterness.

You watched me drown in my turbulent pain,
Because your love for me had already been slain.
I became cold and unforgiving, lost and alone;
Engaging in ways others would never condone.
The pieces of my broken soul are the parts only you can hold,
If you would ever choose to be so bold.
I don't want your hand to save me anymore,
My faith in you has already fallen to the floor.
You led me to drink from your river of deceit.
I dared to believe you were one of the elite.

I continue to embrace my newfound sorrow,
Seeking the promise of a peaceful tomorrow.
Even though I have seen the disappearance of us in your eyes.
I humbly watch the dawn of our demise.
Quietly I will sigh;
As remember you chose to walk through the door of goodbye.

Anyone who claims to be in the light but hates his brother is still in darkness. Whoever loves his brother lives in the light, and there is nothing in him to make him stumble. But whoever hates is brother is in the darkness; he does not know where he is going, because the darkness has blinded him.

1 John 2:9-11 (NIV)

If we want to live in the light, we must forgive and let go of resentments. Humans will engage in behaviors that will hurt us, but we must continue to show the love of Christ in all situations.

SHE

She sits along wayside to make room for the girl
she believes is acceptable, not different.

The sun is darker than the moon in her world.
Yet, she may be the most beautiful girl
you will ever meet and not know it.

She is the mother of beauty.
She is the sister of the strong.
She is the daughter of the meek.

She is the dark beauty who will fade into the wall
in order for someone else to have their moment.

She is mysterious, virtuous, and alone.

Forbearing one another, and forgiving one another, if any man have a quarrel against any: even as Christ forgave you, so also do ye.

Colossians 3:13 (KJV)

Learning to forgive, ourselves first and foremost, is key in letting go of painful memories. The true way to overcome this pain is to forgive, just as Christ forgave us. It is important to remember true forgiveness takes place with the love Christ has instilled in us and not by our might. The only relief from our pain will be abiding in Christ's love and showing His forgiveness. No matter how bad the situation seems, we will only be freed from our life sentence of pain we have given ourselves by forgiving.

THE MOMENT BEFORE DAWN

I watch the moonlight trickle down through the trees,
Soft winds haunt the darkness as they slowly whistle by.
This is the time the world stands still,
It is the moment before dawn.

I close my eyes as I feel alone, the only one with such a struggle.
The gentle ground gives way beneath my feet
and swallows me whole.
I fall to the inner, unexplored portion of my mind.
It is in this place I know I need to change,
lest the venture proves null.
I swiftly criticize the ashes left of my life
and enter the darkest corridor.
I run my hands against the cold, stone walls guarding the pain.
It is an immense fortress placed to protect me from myself;
Yet, I need to conquer it in order to survive.

I pick my head up, with no shame, and stare at the massive walls.
I will surmount my fortress this time.

Rejoice not against me, O mine enemy: when I fall, I shall arise; when I sit in darkness, the Lord shall be a light onto me. I will bear indignation of the Lord, because I have sinned against him until he plead my cause, and execute judgment for me: he will bring me forth to the light, and I shall behold his righteousness.

Micah 7:8-9 (KJV)

The Lord will lead you through the darkness and give you the strength to walk into the light.

I STILL REMEMBER YOU

I look down at my hands as they overflow with my tears;
Reflecting the displaced child, still holding on to translucent fears.
I sit quietly as I look at the despondent wall;
Reminiscent of the moments I have felt I had been through it all.

I now think back to the time I walked with You,
and I would diligently listen to all You had to say;
I somehow let go of Your hand and became lost along the way.
Even though it was I who left, I still remember You.
Father, please bring me home;
I know You think of me, too.

Don't look at me now, children of God,
I'd rather you look away.
I am ashamed because I know I was led astray.
I still think of His presence and I have never been the same.
It hurts so much because I know He has been calling me by name.
It is true; I was mistaken,
but if I return I am so afraid you will judge me.
Please understand I am only crying out
for the One who died to grant *us all* life eternally.

I look up and cry out for the way.
I pray You hear my shout as I say,
"Even though it was I who left, I still remember You."
Father, I know You will bring me home,
because You think of me, too.

What do you think? If a man owns a hundred sheep, and one of them wanders away, will he not leave the ninety-nine on the hills and go look for the one that wandered off? And if he finds it, I tell you the truth, he is happier about that one sheep than about the ninety-nine that did not wander off. In the same way your Father in heaven is not willing that any of these little ones should be lost.

Matthew 18: 12-14 (NIV)

This piece is dedicated to those who have fallen away. The Lord wants us to be with all of us. If at any time we feel the Lord is not there, it is because we have walked away. The Lord will be there if you seek Him, and He will welcome you back with loving arms if you have lost your way. Let no human stand between you and your relationship with Jesus Christ.

VANISH

I once held the flame that shone brightly in the dark,
But sometimes I feel I now only carry a spark.

I try everyday not to vanish into the wall;
I worry about who will catch me if I fall.

It is true; some days I only hear silence.
I can't bear the distance.

Can I truly make it through the night?
Can I peacefully wake to the morning's first light?

I need the armor, but now I feel fragile.
This fading path has been gradual.

Am I living in the shadow and are you the only one I will follow?
Or has my faith become withered and hollow?

I close my eyes and make the effervescent wish;
Lord, please don't let me vanish.

Why are you so downcast, O my soul? Why so disturbed within me? Put your hope in God, for I will yet praise him, my Savior and my God.

Psalm 42:11 (NIV)

Periods of loneliness are usually when God is closest to us. We are never alone and He will never turn His back on us. These are the times we need to seek Him more and He will provide comfort.

SOLEMN GOODBYE

You still clench my wounded heart,
and it is bleeding crimson in your hand.
Through all the hardships,
I thought you to be the one to understand.
You quickly enveloped me with your words and transparent light.
I grasped your hand as you led me away from the darkness of night.

You easily befriended me,
and I entrusted you with the essence of my broken spirit.
But you suddenly turned away and showed no remorse
for discreetly rendering my heart to fragments, bit by bit.
Now you pass me by as though I am not there;
Ensuring the evidence—you never did care.

Has no one told you I am not a stranger and I am not a foe?
All I can say are the words, "We will reap what we sow."
Despite the sadness, I still cared for you sincerely.
My darling, I will admit I have missed you dearly.

However, you have left me no choice but to let you go.
With no more tears, no more regrets, no more sorrow.
I will cherish the brief moments of happiness,
release the bitterness, and again walk with my head held high.
Now all I can say to you from afar,
my dearest one, is my solemn goodbye.

Praise be to the God and Father of our Lord Jesus Christ, the Father of compassion and the God of all comfort, who comforts us in all our troubles, so that we can comfort those in any trouble with the comfort we ourselves have received from God.
2 Corinthians 1:3-4 (NIV)

Saying goodbye is one of the hardest things we can do. In the end, with every goodbye we learn something new. God will comfort us through these times, and then we can extend our gratitude by helping others who may have experienced something similar.

The Loving Embrace

His left hand is under my head, And his right hand embraces me.

Song of Solomon 8:3 (NKJV)

Then you will know the truth, and the truth will set you free.

John 8:32 (NIV)

Finding Jesus Christ is the greatest event that can take place in someone's life. The pieces in this section are called "transition poems." They have this title because these are the first pieces I have ever written with true happiness in the conclusion. Like every poetic sketch in this collection, each one tells a story. Although most of these works begin with darkness, this time there is peace and hope at the end.

This section is about finding the way home and falling into the arms of my Father. The journey finally takes a turn toward a more positive light as the truth about God's love is revealed. The true shedding of darkness takes place poetically in all of the following pieces. And so, as the healing starts to take place, the celebration of the prodigal son's return home begins.

GLASS HEART

I am adrift above my vast ocean of unrealized dreams,
Gazing upon the nighttime moon
as she drops reflections of her silvery beams.
Cold and alone, I close my eyes and imagine
I can transcend above the empty, scattered ashes my life has become.

My thoughts drift away to the vague reality
I am trying to escape from.
The mirror portrays a distorted image of a wounded little girl
who could not find a place to belong.
Her sad, blank stare tells of how she harbors my pain
because I was the one who could not be strong.

Despondency takes my hand and leads me to the place
Where my life was forever changed.
I see the familiar, frail woman desperately on her knees
Because she was the one blamed.
My heart had been shattered, falling to the ground
like broken glass with pieces too sharp to touch.
I quickly tried to mend my heart,
but the jagged edges cut my hands too much.

Tainted and bittersweet, I pressed on,
carefully holding selected fragments left from my heart;
Handing them to anyone who would listen,
in an attempt to keep myself from falling apart.
Even as others taunt out of ignorance,
I once again foolishly chose to place my inclusive trust in someone.
It was too late when I realized
this friendship hurt me more than anyone.

To be continued. . .

The Lord is close to the brokenhearted and saves those who are crushed in spirit.

Psalms 34:18 (NIV)

When most people think of a broken heart, they associate it with failed relationships. Broken hearts can result from anything that deeply hurts us. For example, dreams that remained unfulfilled, so-called failures or the loss of something dear. Allow the Lord to mend your broken heart today.

GLASS HEART (Continued)

Left alone in the cold again to find my own way,
I questioned if it was my fault love refused to stay.
I then walked with a grim, solemn smile
and unshed tears withheld in my eyes;
Seeking shelter behind my fragile, complacent disguise.

I had become nothing but a withered, empty shell.
It was then I realized, on my journey, it was I who fell.
My outstretched arms are reaching out from the valley of the lost;
I once heard the price had been paid,
it was Christ who relieved the cost.

I fell to my knees in shame because of where I had been,
Praying to God, "Father, please forgive my sin."
Christ lifted me tenderly in His loving embrace,
And I gently held the hand of His amazing grace.

He collected the pieces of my broken heart and mended the sorrow;
Giving me the strength to face the dawn of a new tomorrow.
I continue to gravitate toward the perfect love
only Christ can give each time I pray;
Speaking new words of faith I never thought I would say.
Now, despite the trials; I will live, I will love, and I am free.
Because in the end, it was only Christ who could rescue me.

Jesus answered, "I am the way and the truth and the life. No one comes to the Father except through me. If you really knew me, you would know my Father as well. From now on, you do know him and have seen him."

John 14:6 (NIV)

HANDS

My soft screams echo silently throughout time;
Foolishly grieving over what was never mine.
The poverty-stricken child was not deprived of love;
Regret created the fragile armor no one knows of.

I held my final breath in my hands,
Standing on the beach, watching the wind blow over the sands.
You saw me crying over the water, looking at my broken reflection.
You offered shelter from the storm through your divine protection.

Now, instead of holding my final breath close to my heart;
I draw in your breath of life because I know we will never part.
Take my hand and guide through this moment of distress.
Take my heart and release the bitterness.

Make me new, O Lord, help me to forgive.
Thank you for giving me freedom and the chance to finally live.

For I am the Lord, your God, who takes hold of your right hand and says to you. Do not fear; I will help you.

Isaiah 41:13 (NIV)

God cares about you more than anyone ever will. Everyone has experienced brokenness or abandonment at one time or another. God tells us He is there, ready to carry us through.

HERE I AM

Fleeing from the forest, holding images that reflect
the embers of life;
The chains are swift to condemn the 'weak in heart'
to constant, meaningless strife.
Lightning flashes aggressively across the midnight sky.
No longer able to withstand the pain,
I crouch in a corner and solemnly cry.

Can no one see I am dying within?
Drowning in my own pool of conventional sin?
Fear rains down on me like sharp drops of water,
and I eagerly succumb;
Rendering a lifeless smile, feeling jaded, cold, and numb.

I now walk through my placid garden,
praying to God my heart would not harden.
I lift my head and see God's beautiful light.
The darkness surrounding me begins to melt as
He leads me away from the night.
I now willingly embrace His love and my new life.

Cleanse me from uncertainty, and erase from my canvas
of existence all the heartfelt strife.
I will no longer wade through my field of tears:
Christ has removed my transparent fears.

Here I am;
Following as childlike and innocent as possible,
engaged in prayer for the lost.
Lord, help us reach out and tell what you have done for us,
How you fulfilled the cost.

But be sure to fear the Lord and serve him faithfully with all your heart; consider what great things he has done for you.

1 Samuel 12:24 (NIV)

Jesus Christ is the only one who can save us. It is through Him, and only Him, that we have our salvation and peace of mind. He can heal the emotional pain and depression.

THE DARKNESS

Following the false gust of wind as it leads me in the wrong direction.
In the breeze, I thought myself to see my true reflection.
Can anyone see me or hear my voice screaming for peace?
I've endured the pain I thought would never cease.

The darkness began to invade my heart;
Slowly I could feel myself falling apart.
I know I am not unique in what I feel;
I know many experience the same type of ordeal.

I was dying within but I remembered Jesus Christ had died for my sin.
I still turned my head; choosing my burdens instead.

No one truly knows my life and why I made this choice.
I have lived a life of disarray, but still ignored his voice.
Before long, my world and soul became broken.
I remembered the whisper of Jesus and
the words just as they were spoken.

He accepted me, despite the life I led.
And now I live by every word He has said.
As the darkness tried to seep to my soul, clearly I see;
He is the only one who could deliver light to the dark side of me.

Then they cried to the Lord in their trouble, and he saved them from their distress. He brought them out of darkness and the deepest gloom and broke away their chains.

Psalms 107:13-14 (NIV)

Despite our situations and no matter how dark they appear, Christ is the only one who can take us away from the darkness, the depression, the loneliness, and the lack of peace. He can break all of the chains and strongholds in anyone's life.

LORD, HEAR MY CRY

I am drowning in my tears as they have created an infinite ocean.
I've been overtaken by my thoughtless emotion.

The feelings taunt me and try to take me captive.
I reach out because I am just trying to live.

Show me the power of Your hand.
Help me understand.

Take from me these thoughts of inequity;
Open my eyes and reveal the light to me.

I just want to seek you.
Lord; I want to be filled with your words, too.

I want to melt in your presence.
I want to bathe in your essence.

Lord, hear my cry.
Save me from myself and the visual lie.

I want this to be a true love story;
Only you can save me.

For you did not receive the spirit of bondage again to fear, but you received the Spirit of adoption by whom we cry out, "Abba, Father."

Romans 8:15

He hears us when we cry out and is there with open arms.

LOOK

An angry rose forced to bloom;
Look within and feel her gloom.

The thunder rages from the storm outside;
Look down and release your pride.

The eagle will continue to soar;
Look up, extend your hand, reach for more.

The wind in the distant forest will continue to sing;
Look around at the joy you can help bring.

Thank you, Lord, for all you are and all you do.
If we **look deep** we will find our true reflection lies in you.

I have been crucified with Christ and I no longer live, but Christ lives in me. The life I live in the body, I live by faith in the Son of God, who loved me and gave himself for me.

Galatians 2:20 (NIV)

When we truly surrender our lives to God and accept Jesus Christ into our hearts, His love is reflected through us if we allow it to flow.

THE CANDLE

It's been years since the light of my candle has died.
It was hard to keep it burning, but God knows how hard I tried.
My candle was quenched by the turbulent tide washing in over me,
Bringing with it damage as far as the eye could see.

Left to collect the pieces of my dreams littered across the land;
In this dark moment, God's love gently took me by the hand.
Now the flood has ended, and I see the rainbow up above;
Transforming the hatred my spirit seemed to have been composed of.

I know He has created me with innate love in my soul.
My reunion with God has made me whole.
Now I can say when I look in the mirror, I see a reflection of Him.
The candle within my soul is no longer dim.

For thou wilt light my candle: the Lord my God will enlighten my darkness.

Psalm 18:28 (KJV)

God is the only one who can fill the void we all feel. He will light our candle of life, and we will keep it burning through obedience.

I AM NOT ALONE

I am not the person I was yesterday;
I am not the person I will be tomorrow;
I am who I am today only through Christ,
Because He has lifted the secluded sorrow.

Love has now become my companion;
Solace I finally was able to befriend;
Truth always stands by my side;
Euphoric bliss too intricate to comprehend.

My salvation illustrates all things are possible through Christ;
My blood no longer gleams with pain against the snow.
I stand as a new Child of God before you;
Expressing love I never thought I could show.

My soul is no longer withered from the storm,
My heart no longer made of stone.
The undertone of sadness and loneliness has dissipated
as I walk in the light of Christ.
I am not alone.

Therefore if any man be in Christ, he is a new creature: old things are passed away; behold, all things are become new.

2 Corinthians 5:17 (KJV)

Although I am just in the beginning of my rebirth in God, He views me as a new creation and His loving child. Although obedience is vital, God's love is not determined by works. He will love us continually. It is us who need to remain faithful.

Walking in the Light

The people walking in darkness have seen a great light; on those living in the land of deep darkness a light has dawned.

Isaiah 9:2 (NIV)

For God, who said, "Let light shine out of darkness," made his light shine in our hearts to give us the light of the knowledge of the glory of God in the face of Christ.

2 Corinthians 4:6 (NIV)

The last section of poetic sketches is a thank you to my Lord Jesus Christ. The pieces describe light, and the darkness has been lifted. Some are dedicated to worship while others describe life in the light. Overall, the message is about love, joy, and adoration for God.

On a final note, this has been a long journey because change does not occur overnight. I am still growing each day and learning to live in the light. When behaviors are so engrained, even positive change can take a while to adjust to. If you choose to embark on your own journey because you are tired of living in the dark and you identify with the life the pieces describe, remember patience and endurance are important to sustain the changes. God will help you if you allow Him to. Believe change is possible and that life does not have to be painful.

NOW

The power of God is apparent;
Through the transformation from darkness to light.
Replacing the deepest of sorrows with strength,
Which had been just beyond grasp,
Taking away blindness and providing newfound sight.

Now...
I drink from your presence because this is my water.
I feed from your word because this is my bread.
I am covered by your blood because this is my salvation.
Your Holy Spirit I will follow because this is how I am led.

Now...
The joy of the Lord reaches out to others from my spirit.
My eyes render the reflection of the Son.
His presence and faithfulness create the atmosphere of my life—
All evidence I am a child of the Holy One.

But the hour is coming, and now is, when the true worshipers will worship the Father in spirit and truth; for the Father is seeking such to worship Him. God *is* Spirit, and those who worship Him must worship in spirit and truth.

John 4:23-24 (NKJV)

We were created to worship and fellowship with God.

THE SON IS IN MY EYES

As I lift His name up,
I bow my head and offer words of worship.

I think of His mercy upon me, and on my knees I quickly fall;
Crystal tears of bliss drip from my face when I think of it all.

I know the rebirth of my soul has just begun,
But He has already deemed me a new creation.

I am now free to worship in spirit;
The one whose power is infinite.

God has allowed me to see;
I no longer need to believe the visual lies,
Because now, the Son is in my eyes.

The Spirit of God, who raised Jesus from the dead, lives in you. And just as God raised Christ Jesus from the dead, he will give life to your mortal bodies by this same Spirit living within you.

Romans 8:11 (NLT)

Once we accept Jesus Christ as Lord of our life, it is no longer about us but about Christ who dwells in us.

My Prayer

As we walk the path of faith you have set before us each day,
May your mercy and grace illuminate our hearts along the way.

Your radiance and complexity are beyond all reason;
Your love will always be with us for more than just a season.

May words of worship and gratitude softly drip from our lips,
As we reach to the heavens and
grasp your presence with our fingertips.

Enrapture us, O Lord, with your beautiful splendor and majesty.
In awe, we close our eyes and bow before your resonating glory.

The most beautiful aspect is the fact
that you know us all individually;
Evidenced as you gave your life just to be with each of us eternally.

Take me as I am; I offer myself in sweet surrender.
My lord, this is my prayer.

Then you will call upon me and come and pray to me, and I will listen to you.

Jeremiah 29:12 (NIV)

Prayer is our definitive fellowship with God. He will always be available to listen because His faithfulness is unwavering.

MY BEAUTIFUL KING

I want to lift my hands in praise to you.
My lord, all things in my life have become new.
I want to lift my voice in song of praise.
You have forgiven and forgotten the sin of my previous days.

Lead me, and I will follow; I will worship; I will sing,
"Glory to my beautiful King!"

I want to witness your magnificence and majesty
And feel your presence rush over me.
With each passing day,
I want my love for you to grow more and more.
Lord, that I may one day see you in your entire splendor.

Lead me, and I will follow; I will worship: I will sing,
"Glory to my beautiful King!"

Glory and honor to God forever and ever! He is the eternal King, the unseen one who never dies; he alone is God. Amen.

1 Timothy 1:17 (NLT)

God, our Father, is the true eternal King. He deserves all the honor and the glory we have to offer. Also recognize that when you enter this family through Jesus Christ, you are also a child of the King.

SERVANT

Take me away from all that I am;
Let me see the power of the Lamb.

Take all selfish thoughts and release me from my life.
Show me the healing power you have over all strife.

Mold me as you would clay;
Reveal your Holy Way.

Let your Holy Spirit rain down on me.
I want to be closer to spending life with you eternally.

I want this to be about sweet surrender—
Spending life together.

I want to be a living sacrifice.
Because I know just part of my heart does not suffice.

I want to fall in love with all that you are.
I never want to feel too far.

Lord, be with me, walk with me, and talk with me,
For I am your willing servant perpetually.

Bring joy to your servant, for to you, O Lord, I lift up my soul.

Psalm 86:4 (NIV)

Christ first gave us the example of becoming a servant. Likewise, we should be a servant to the Lord.

THANK YOU NOTE

Dear Lord,
You are my Life, my Love, and my King.
This is my thank you note for your everlasting love and blessing.

Each one of your children
has something special to present to you—
Everyone different in their gratitude,
mostly dependent upon what you have carried them through.

As we continue to live this life filled with good and evil,
both of which we must discern;
Lord, we will continue to do your will
as we patiently await your promised return.

My Lord, my God, I just want to send you this
'Thank You Note' to let you know;
I think of you wherever I am, wherever I go.

I will continually give thanks to The Most High; The Perfect One;
My Redeemer; God's Only Son.

I will thank you, Lord, with all my heart; I will tell of all the marvelous things you have done.

Psalm 9:1 (NLT)

I give thanks for everything in my life, especially the transformation from darkness to light. This change did not occur over night. Just as the sun rises slowly and sheds light, so is it with our changes. They can be slow, but once the sun rises our darkness disappears. It is well worth the journey and the patience to receive a new life without depression or darkness.

THE ROAD

Walking along the dusty, winding road,
Leaving behind the example of love He showed.
To the people He was a mystery.
The miracles left several saying, "How could this be?"
Loved by many, despised by some,
The Son of God had finally come.
Although He spoke the truth in all He would do,
The end of the day drew near, but only He knew.

Persecuted and battered,
Left alone because, in fear, His disciples scattered.
As He faced the prosecution,
He was sentenced to the cruelest execution.
With nails driven through His hands
and a crown of thorns upon His head,
Many mocked Him as He suffered, and His blood was shed.

The Scripture now fulfilled as the world suffered the great loss;
It was our sin that placed Jesus Christ upon that cross.
That day my Savior died in such a brutal way,
But He overcame the grave on the third day.
He died for you and me to be forgiven; today He lives,
But it's your choice to take the road to the eternal life He gives.

For God so loved the world that he gave his one and only Son, that whoever believes in him shall not perish but have eternal life.

John 3:16 (NIV)

Jesus Christ died for all of our sins. He is the Son of God who loves us so much he suffered a cruel death in order for us to be with him eternally. Our life on earth can be difficult, but change in anyone's life is possible through the power of Jesus Christ. He lives today, and if you want him to live in your heart, pray this prayer:

Father, I thank you for sending your Son Jesus Christ to die for my sins. Jesus, I open my heart and invite you in. I accept you as my Savior and confess you as Lord of my life. Help me to prevail over the sin in my life, to do Your will and to obey You. In the name of Jesus I pray, Amen.

If you have prayed this prayer, find fellowship with other believers and read the Holy Bible. Rely on God for the guidance to take the next steps of your new life.

AWAKEN THE TRUTH

I have walked under the weight of my transgression;
Bound by the indescribable and set free by the Son of God Himself.
The age old adversary is circling, to and fro;
searching for a stronghold by which to bind the young and old.
The accuser of the Brethren disguises himself
among those we love;
Just think of people documented in the Word of God;
Cain and Abel, Joseph and his brothers, Samson and Delilah,
and most the most famous (who betrayed the Son of God
with a kiss on the cheek) Judas Iscariot and Jesus Christ.

Satan attacked the first family
and tainted the creation that brings God joy.
He continues to do so today, with age-old tactics.
Love your brother and sister.
Every human on earth is your family under God.

We truly do not fight against flesh and blood, this is Biblical.

"For we do not wrestle against flesh and blood,
but against principalities,
against powers, against the rulers of the darkness of this age,
against spiritual hosts of wickedness
in the heavenly places." (Ephesians 6:12)

We fight against all the dark forces that use people,
and most do not even know it.
These are the forces who seek to destroy us as humans.

We are given a choice- Accept Jesus Christ and be obedient or suffer eternal separation from the Godhead-Abba Father, Jesus Christ, and the Holy Spirit. This means complete loss of love, joy, peace, and everything God offers. The opposite is pain, misery, guilt, fear, and loneliness...for eternity. Will you risk that?

We were bought with a price-the life of the only sinless man ever born and the only sinless spirit released from a human to enter eternity, Jesus Christ. "For you were bought at a price; therefore glorify God in your body and in your spirit, which are God's."

(Corinthians 6:20 NKJV)

We were warned-"Nor give place to the devil."

(Ephesians 4:27 NKJV)

We were instructed-"Submit yourselves to God, resist the devil and he will flee from you."

(James 4:7 NKJV)

"[18.] And Jesus came and spoke to them, saying, "All authority has been given to Me in heaven and on earth.[19.] Go therefore and make disciples of all the nations, baptizing them in the name of the Father and of the Son and of the Holy Spirit,[20.] teaching them to observe all things that I have commanded you; and lo, I am with you always, even to the end of the age." Amen."

(Matthew 28:18-20 NKJV)

We were promised-Jesus Christ (King of Kings and Lord of Lords) will come a second time.

"[11.]Now I saw heaven opened, and behold, a white horse. And He who sat on him *was* called Faithful and True, and in righteousness He judges and makes war. [12] His eyes *were* like a flame of fire, and on His head *were* many crowns. He had a name written that no one knew except Himself. [13] He *was* clothed with a robe dipped in blood, and His name is called The Word of God. [14] And the armies in heaven, clothed in fine linen, white and clean, followed Him on white horses. [15] Now out of His mouth goes a sharp sword, that with it He should strike the nations. And He Himself will rule them with a rod of iron. He Himself treads the winepress of the fierceness and wrath of Almighty God. [16] And He has on *His* robe and on His thigh a name written:

KING OF KINGS AND LORD OF LORDS."

Revelations 19:11-16 (NKJV)

Seek God, be ready...No one is promised tomorrow and He IS coming back.

About the Author

Nancy L. Martinez currently resides in Chimayo, New Mexico. She holds a Masters in Bilingual/Bicultural Clinical Social Work, and is an Independent Mental Health Therapist. She has devoted her life to supporting and helping people who are afflicted with mental illness and emotional difficulties. She has also been honored on the National Wall of Tolerance in Alabama, and has received many different recognitions over the last 17 years for her commitment to humanity.

You may contact her with questions of emotional healing through Jesus Christ via messaging, and receive current articles written by her at: http://www.facebook.com/inspire.faith.nm